Freeschoolin': The 1 Rule Of Freeschoolin' Is There Are No Rules To Freeschoolin'!

Written and Illustrated by Wendy Elizabeth Hart

Dedicated to my parents whom without I would not be here.

Thankful for all your lessons, love and help.

Love you forever.

Freeschoolin': The 1 Rule Of Freeschoolin' Is There Are No Rules To Freeschoolin'!
Freeschoolin' Series Book 2
Text and Illustrations copyright © Wendy Elizabeth Hart

Editing by Jaze Hart.

©2022 All rights reserved.

No part of this publication may be reproduced, stored in a retrieval system or transmitted in any form or by any means, electronic, mechanical photocopying, recording or otherwise, without prior written permission of Hart2Hart Art Publishing
Email – horsewhisperer333@hotmail.com

First Edition

ISBN 978-0-9959219-5-5 (pbk.)

Published By Hart2Hart Art Publishing

Freeschoolin': The 1 Rule Of Freeschoolin' Is There Are No Rules To Freeschoolin'!

Written and Illustrated by Wendy Elizabeth Hart

Hi! My Name is Hope
and I am 7 years old.

The one rule of
Freeschoolin' is there are
NO RULES to
Freeschoolin'!

Freeschoolin'

In our home, we respect each other's boundaries and limitations.

No rules needed.

My parents keep me safe
as I learn about the
world.

Safety is an important
boundary.

I am learning how to respect others because I am respected.

Time
WAITS
for
NO ONE

I like making healthy food choices.

I am never pressured.

My Parents model and encourage healthy habits.

My body is my own to care for.

I decide my style.

My family happily supports my choices.

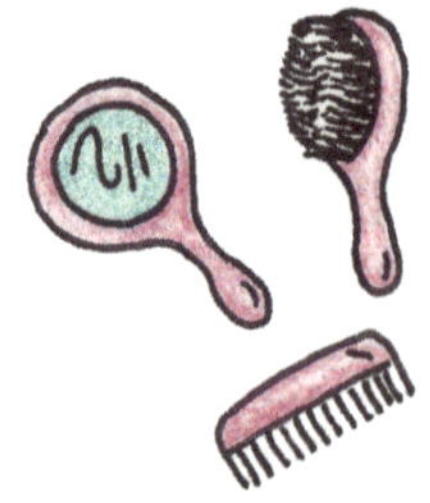

I love learning because
I am free to follow my
interests each day.

ABC
S
1 cup
HOPE
1 2 3
PAINT

Together our family makes plans, talks about issues and shares feelings.

We are a community.

I am always listened to,
so I find I can listen to
others.

I choose my own bedtime.

I always wake up rested
and ready for my day.

"Please's" and "Thank You's" come from my heart.

They are never expected or forced.

PLEASE
Thank · You
please
THANKS

These are the reasons that...

The one rule of Freeschoolin' is there are NO RULES to

I ♥ YOU

About the Author

Wendy Elizabeth Hart is a grateful Mom of two, a talented professional artist, married to her best friend, living an unschooled, homesteading life.

Through observing her family learning from living everyday, Wendy was inspired to share their passion-led, wholesome life in the Freeschoolin' Children's Book Series.

"Thank you for being a part of our Freeschoolin' journey. Much Love Always. "-Wendy Elizabeth Hart